TRANSNATIONAL
MUSCLE
CARS

Jeff Derksen

Talonbooks

2003

Talonbooks
P.O. Box 2076, Vancouver, British Columbia, Canada V6B 3S3
www.talonbooks.com

Typeset in Janson and printed and bound in Canada.

First Printing: June 2003

National Library of Canada Cataloguing in Publication Data

Derksen, Jeff, 1958-
 Transnational muscle cars / Jeff Derksen.

 A poem.
 ISBN 0-88922-473-0

 I. Title.
PS8557.E5895T72 2003   C811'.54   C2003-910128-2
PR9199.3.D454T72 2003

The publisher gratefully acknowledges the financial support of the Canada
Council for the Arts; the Government of Canada through the Book
Publishing Industry Development Program; and the Province of British
Columbia through the British Columbia Arts Council for our publishing
activities.

ACKNOWLEDGEMENTS

This book was a long time coming, so various versions, rewrites and differently titled works that ultimately ended up in this book were published in: *Arras, Bombay Gin, Canadian Literature, Crayon, dandelion, DC Poetry, The East Village, Essex, filling station, hunch, The Literary Review* ("Global New York"), *Object, Open Letter, The Queen Street Quarterly, Philly Talks, Raddle Moon, side/lines: a new canadian poetics, Site Street, Sulphur, XCP: Cross-Cultural Poetics*. Thanks to the editors for their support of this work. Thanks too, go to the many places where readings provided a vital public platform and staging ground for these texts: Zinc Bar, Segue Series @ Double Happiness, The Drawing Center (NYC); The Kootenay School of Writing (Vancouver); Banff Centre for the Arts, The New Gallery (Calgary); DCAC (Washington, DC); The Poetics Program of SUNY Buffalo; Redhead Gallery, Scream in High Park (Toronto); Universidade de Vigo, Spain; University of Minnesota; Sub Text Series (Seattle); Small Press Traffic (San Francisco); and Platform Gallery (London).

But Could I Make a Living from It (in a different form) was published as a hole chapbook. Thanks to Louis Cabri and Rob Mannery. Parts of that poem were also used in the film *What Is Left?* by Penelope Buitenhuis.

This book is the outcome of the interaction of many people, cities and "spaces of hope." Tip of the iceberg: Louis Cabri, Kevin Davies, Sianne Ngai, Rodrigo Toscano, Brian Kim Stefans, Fred Wah, Kelly Wood, The Center for Place, Culture and Politics and The Social Mark. Thanks as well to Bart Lootsma and Helmut Weber of the Lorenz Mandl Gasse team and to my transnational roomate, Mark Nowak. The dedication of this book is (as my previous book is), sadly, to the dead, but the writing is for the living: For Sabine Bitter.

The author wishes to recognize funding from the Canada Council and the Alberta Foundation for the Arts for their economic support of culture, including this book.

for H. L. Derksen
1929–2001

*But we cannot make either our history or our geography
under historical-geographical conditions of our own choosing.*
—David Harvey, *Spaces of Hope*

*… because capitalism makes the nouns
and burns the connections …*
—Bob Perelman, *First World*

Jerk

The sun glints off the chrome bodies
of the gondolas of late capitalism
as they labour up the mountain.
The mountain is named
after a commodity. Art has made this
a nonalienated view. Is that what
we asked it to do? If "each day seems
like a natural fact" and if "what we think
changes how we act" should art not
reveal ideology
rather than naturalize it?

These old idealisms, they burn me up
These old idealisms, what do they cover up?

You had a lovely critique
and you looked great, sexy
really, the way your world-market
pants might shock the bourgeoisie
into consciousness. But these days
I'm yearning not for a little outside
to call homeland, although I like good
design too and do feel that "workers"
(morphed "multitude") also live
outside of quotation marks
in this "the highest stage"—

but now I'm wanting transformation
rather than "structural adjustment"
to go with the primitive accumulation
and worn contradictions. Not more
of these natural facts ("globalization is").

But back to this "ocularcentric" art
as social goggles, the artist
as opthamologist. I want to see
the real relations
but you've got Nikes on and I like you
so I have to try and understand. And if
that shirt's from The Gap, then one arm was sewn
in Malaysia, the other in Sri Lanka. Why then
is it hard to "see" ideology when you're
wearing it? Is it "out there"? Or deeper inside
than even desire could get? That clarity
would lead to historical consciousness
is muddied to the point
where you wouldn't even recognize
your buddies once you got there. "Hey you
Louis!" (There is history
to spontaneity, anger, irony).
"People have opinions / where
do they come from?" My idealistic belief
is that historical consciousness may come.
My sad cognitive mapping
is that overdetermined contradictions
don't lead to new social relations.
I want an art
more complicated than that.

Happy Locally, Sad Geopolitically

The misery of millionaires
shows it is a classless society.
It's harder to be happy
geopolitically
so new restaurants are reviewed
quickly before they close. "Strange to"
remember or reach a point
past when I had more nouns
in my life than pronouns
but that's just capitalism's way
of saying "I hear you knocking, but
you can't come in." So stranger still
that there has not been an immediate
poll to polarize positions.
But here I merely
talk to myself as if all
is textual, as if I am a lyricist
of late capitalism (or Dig
The New Imperialism)
ambling in the streets
of a fin-de-siècle city
fixed in the fingers of inevitability
and the gloomy vision
of the centre right
(air tight) and anachronistic
nation-states (festering hyphen)
backed up by all

the lovely possible positions
we can come to understand (slack
out). I now address the "bifurcation
of space" as the world is anew
in old relations that drop like a half-sack
of part-time jobs into your lap
(did I mention that global pleasures
are few and hard to talk to?)
Dipping into the notebooks
of the past, where firm beliefs (firm's
belief) are up for loan (loam)
or are an approach
to products
(formerly "things" not "relations")
tear ducts taped up
with duct tape. All week saints die
which will help Elton John
and the flower exports
of Tenerife. Dad, the car is screaming
in an uncanny return
of cams as if I can
feel the metal sizzle
of short on top, long on
the back. I've arranged
a clean modernist bargain
injection-molded plastic space
to work in. It's uneven
development without the human
edge: you can't ask so don't
ask. Suharto pepper spray
competition (his son's

on the run). Still planes rise
and merge, slide down corridors
of nonplaces to natural
unemployment levels
slaking generational
career expectations (sloth) across
borders through which people pour
(the politics of
water). The trade irritant
of wood (culture), an Expo, world-class
huckster hoopla penetrated
by a pencil. Balanced by practical
fanny packs for mini-van nights
on the highway to
bilingual roadsigns.
Don't Hilfiger my hegemony
with paper. Drippy pavilion
paved with anvils and the anger
of all the urbanists bundled
into a bundle of broken
previous "textures" and the good
life stuff of living Alzheimers. Come
feel the malice
as town planning
bursts from a psycho-
pathology of a mayor
in the discourse of dimes. Don't
spit from the viewing platform
for heroes. I take that as
an insult to my own brand
of hostile stupidity that I have bred

in the petri dish of anxieties
cut free of economic determinism—you
vulgar glaring rung nudger! Now
that Algeria alters
France's social space
something's gotta give! Writing
can no longer be daily mind mapping
as it was once so easy
to please with point by point
hits (power point). Let's go Toronto
Jumbotron! (a nation mourns, a city
is supersized). To placate a deeper
description a bitterness shared
between friends (hosed over
after) carried through the years
patched up through emerging
technology and plummeting
long distance rates. It's an aching slow burn
why "deficits are unethical"
and surplus is celebrated
not celibate—but better than
Martha Stewart Lifestyles International
when the stocks
are down. But a worn (warm)
swarm cuts the last
limp into eligibility and ligit mimicry
cries out of a pout. Reach out and
salt the wound—that's what good
corporate neighbours are for! A little bit country
a little bit button-down (whose
kind of town). Dear dreaded enemies

powerful neighbours, cultural buddies, product
knock-offs in whose house
I dwell, send the cheque in Euros
or I'll kill myself and then
slash your tires chronologically
to counter gestures
down the wing
into a neutral space trap (neural). Never
trust the driver—he's drunk
or power blind like a pig
with pork. The human sparkplug
of radical civic engineering
requests a pluralism (team logos)
in the projects: bring in
the middle class! Applause in the
transcript for Fidel
in Harlem and "new world
international economic order"
speech. Now that the patriotic right
has taken over even the "radicality" of shopping
which held so much hope (united
sweaters). I live where anti-freeze was
sweeter than wine. How whales
"make their living." Strip mall
bricolage logic is traveling culture
(refuted in subsequent essays). I'm
trying to work against (within)
how this city (boom) humbles
humans as ornaments. Lowest per capita
can't be beat. Awful
architecture. Carried like eggs

in your wallet. Where can
we get an Ireland? In the tension
between universalism
and particularism
there's an impulse
to buy not sell. Real relations
hover over workers'
gloves on stones of Expos
inflated in Osaka. Work is done
as if by itself and returns
as something alien: imagine saying "I
made that toilet paper!" The song
now becomes beautiful
as determinations move
toward blunted bans
on foot-activated shrapnel.
How is this "my world"
any more than the typeface
of the Boston Pizza logo (mimetic)
or the eggman (realism) of Humpty's Family
Restaurant? Is it because
I hate you that I
think of you? Are pronouns
rude or just unfair? The alleys (elegies)
filled with crappy cars, a rusted out
Monte Carlo with Cragar
mags, mattresses, the imprint
of a dumpster burnt
into the dirt, that's
entertainment. In the summit
for funds, grassroots juvenile

detention camps to supplement
the tourist economy like leakage
or trickle-down to lower (the effluent
society!). "Skateboarders
are people too!" Looking
good! Good design! Goodbye
Kyoto Accord, Honda Accord!
Upper-case me dot
so I can get "the fuck
out of this town" via pavement
and crooked rain. I'm doing
a total Yeltsin to intercept
this broadcast for a message
from my liver, from a modernism
when bodies could talk
and say something like
"the age of." With air conditioning
$298 a month and a pack
of Galloise. Memorial police
helicopter thumps. Third International
Brotherhood of Grinders.
Now that an Algerian-born
footballer alters France's
cultural space he has become
a genius! Boom, a town
amongst "jittery Asian markets," as "Russia
unravels" correlated
with the return of "cronyism"
and classic cocktails: rusty
nail, manhattan, whisky
sour, and the social acceptance

of the crantini. Clean
sightlines, Bauhaus bathrooms. Korea
(which one) is tricky. The Duma
is acceptable. Currency, it cancels
us. I'm harping, I'm
thematic, hit me with
a study guide! Go
gothic! The ads are compelling
in that they speak to me. Affairs (flairs)
of men like he is drunk
on the power of potatoes
(when I say "potato," I mean
"vodka," when I say
"vodka," I mean
"fictive ethnicities" on ice). Is there now
a place for outrage, a glaze for lags, a
flag for flack. Distinguish (extinguish)
ourselves on the world stage imperative
from the faceoff. Forget 68, you sixty-eighters
remember 73! "Two choices," we need
you now (it's not just a revolution
you can dance papier mâché to). World
service summaries tool each day
to awake bully bearish bound
to unseen forces that, to quote
the poet, linger like liquor
on the breath of the portrayal
of former Soviet leaders. That said, join
me in front of the cold screen
for hot media as "the tip
of the iceberg" from

"Teenage Tina." Judo, yes
Judo. Transient "cultural workers" reunite
for might (*dwell* magazine's "A Year
in the Life of Nomads" map). In this
sweaty sexualized struggle
of the lowdown and the local
where discounts
are deeper elsewhere
dialects dial in and insurgent
architecture answers. Concrete and glass
it's a class, class, class. Which may ask
can we really know all this
relativism or even
the Swiss? "Speedskaters
of former Yugoslavia
unite under the flag
of fetishwear for return of the
repossessed post-NATO realignment
lines combined with panic-attack
currency kebabs" is the kind
of sentence I am thinking
about. From the excesses
of my youth to the excuses
of both, to free-floating formal quotations
little moments of appropriated
pleasure are nowhere near
enough to be filled with alarm
of life lived to max capacity
that others recognize
where democracy dwells
demos of singular stand-ins. Radial

not radical! In these internationalist
moments I open my stylish arms
to you as a gesture
of "hey man" that you
don't have to leave the house for
as long as the goods (spackle, salt
salsa, concrete poetry, video clips, particular
olive oil, bootleg Chinese CDs
that threaten an emerging market, preselected
wine delivery, halogen bulbs, tansy buttons,
pure products gone goofy
on behalf of world citizens
fully represented and ready
to go with interventionalist billboard
projects. When the world
intrudes on you
is it "the world"
or the sharp shapes of early determinants
mom's refusal, dad's approval
or vise versa with the kindly
or harsh grandmother, summers
in nature and urban winters
then on to your studies duties
classical philosophy (music)
arise now as "key" negotiating
points in the contract (contact)
of "all that is you"
interiorized and made material
in labour. My friends, my
endorphins. I'm drying out, help
me to Hyundai a website

such as "Sven's Canada Page" or "Opel
Manta Through History." At last
(least) that's a surplus-value self
you could spread around.
My grandmother's vodka pneumonia
is settler literature
curriculum reevaluation
and immigration is narrative's
unmoored rumours
of more. Getting beaten
with a long rubber hose
is an innovation of flexi post-
Fordism. Jerk!
Chicken! These
missed moments of capitalism
like a detective novel
for development. Better, is he drunk
or just a business man
with plural futures? (paid plaid.) Said
the new human mayoral candidate
to the megacity. Cuban pajamas
in Wal-Mart make me bring it on home
in that pick-up (purple and mine
because he died.) What makes you
think you can behave
like the sole superpower? (Oh, don't
be embarrassed). To vote, think
only of yourself
in relation to
yourself, others
are fucked

so fuck them (also helpful
for the workplace). But tomorrow
is a new day of entry-level middle-brow
appreciation formerly called "culture"
now a.k.a. "polish my pistons loser."
And the return
of quiz shows as Super Suds
community building. *Rambo 1: First Blood* was filmed
in the small B.C. town
where my grandparents farmed rocks
and bootlegged fish, now I live
in the nation-state origin of Arnold
Schwarzenegger, although I can't
support his presidency.
Hipster pumps and
corporate humps. Exaggerated American
leisure, detonated tonalities ting
a roti (etceteras). The leading wedge
of baby strollers and the barge
of twin bundles. I have dwelt in the
felt of feelings and felt
the weight of dwelling, now
the blight of bleakness
is less than the atonal noodlings
of a bubbly Eno
which spring into melody
often "surprising (to their
originators) and inventive fashions."
Is it the rub of culture that blisters
or just the newfound possibilities
of ticks and ties

and DJ kicks
when it gets so easy
to universalize? (fly flicked into
keyboard, "heart burst
in the back of a taxi.)" My own
nationalist thought is flooded with diodes
and odes at odds with the complex
bracketed connectivity vital
extensions sent to futuristic
cities of bubbles, globes and domes
hotwaxed to our decks.
My journey wearies me
(man!) thus I dock
in your city to take provisions
of new music, books and clothes
before I move on to lands
as yet untapped
or tapped on the shoulder
by primitive accumulation
with the timelessness
of Cat Stevens (circa *Harold and Maude*)
and with the sadness of architects
who watch homes built
without them. The bar
is lowered, the light is bent
we live out lives singularly
in a time of
close
quotes.

But Could I Make a Living From It

That's a nice sunset you have there.

I'm three years younger than the term *Third World*.

This is where your body goes after you donate it to "medical research."

I'm a cultural nationalist waiting to happen.

"Note: these awards are custom made to individual requirements and are NOT mass-produced."

This landscape demands another attention span that mediates me flatly and broadly.

It's the apex where sexuality's spliced in.

Do you really want to use it that way, I mean to use it?

The sun reflects off the triangular glass tower downtown and into my bed—I sprawl on this corporate light.

"Writing can be no more definitive than can one's place in history."

Just don't touch me during the drum solo.

Trees are cod.

Outside of a metaphor I have a body, but as a statistic I can at least show up on a bar graph.

1976: 0.9861.

"Land Rover owners go on forever."

Canadian dollar?

But the city is an urban mistake imposed on a place that makes sense—a monument to a certain model of history.

By this I mean I'll take the bigger one and put it on my card.

Afghanistan, Angola, Bangladesh, Benin.

To be in the "world" in the position of quotation marks.

I would rather have your fingers in my mouth than "find my own voice."

"Mr. X, a capitalist who produces woolen yarn in his spinning mill, has to 'reproduce' his raw material …. "

Grass is trees.

This "transaction" translates me until I become my own ethnographic smear.

A tendency to read all languages as anagrams of English—as slang gauges.

"The flow of thought is not accompanied by a simultaneous unfolding of speech."

The corporate core without a body.

I respond with managerial skills, organizing differences into discourses.

If white people can find one another exotic, that's how I find you.

The kind of consumer support of the Third World.

And a rusty gas barbeque on every balcony.

Something deep inside "synchronic ethnographic liberalism" says "Can I borrow that for a minute?"

"A colleague of mine insists the color of a man's watchband should match that of his belt and shoes: Who is correct?"

Bhutan, Burkina Faso, Burundi, Cambodia.

Porque soy Jeff, hijo de mi madre.

He carefully explained his "I'm so privileged that now I'm marginalized" position to me.

"Let us now return to Hegel."

Walking, drunk with a cup, it's nationhood.

Leisure is just organized production.

A proud yet flexible and disposable worker.

"On the other hand many well-intentioned people have resisted jumping on the guilt bandwagon for lack of convincing data."

In the morning I want a voice to attenuate touch.

"Uninhibited working-class sexuality" in the basement.

Technicians of the Abbreviated.

1978: 1.1402.

It's not that the content is mine, but that it has been made generic.

Bright yellow label.

Cape Verde, Central African Republic, Chad, Comoros.

"Mr. Y, a heavy engineer producing machine-tools …. "

False centre of accusation with moral funding (more war!).

I become a "world citizen" with the arrival of my phone card.

Investment banking as a sexual term.

Post-Desert Storm tumours.

That's law suits to you.

I'll stand in for form, for me.

It's the "political economy of genitals" that puts us inside production.

Desire's tendon tightens.

Bootstraps will pull me up through the masses, classes.

I could use a bit of that "privileging of the proletariat" every now and then.

Just how are you replicated in architecture?

Autonomous condo.

I am the same age as Mies van der Rohe's Seagram Building.

"You can now capitalize on emerging markets and Latin America from just £30 a month."

Retired General "Stormin'" Norman Schwarzkopf undergoes prostate surgery.

The plane drops into a cartoon version of heaven.

1980: 1.1690.

"Money traders and ordinary people."

Tourism as a method of state control for both the tourists and the hosts.

In my name an anagram for an act.

From the air, the canals are darker, crooked roads.

Why don't you "master" your own culture first?

Democratic Republic of Congo, Djibouti, Equatorial Guinea, Eritrea.

"At some point in my life I became obsessed with having just the right wristwatch."

So-called maleness, so-called critical investigation.

Upper-class classism versus working-class racism.

"Latin America: Rich in History   Resource   Potential."

I'll quietly wait for my big break.

Good morning little graduate schoolboy.

If only we could elevate poetry to pop culture—smells like corporate spirit.

To give this a context, I'm writing below sea level, but I don't know what time it is and I don't speak the language.

1982: 1.2341.

Any mood-altering substance please.

It's erotic to say everything, but let's just do this and talk later.

"Possible military intervention" so people can live "ordinary lives."

If only the rich people could see us now!

Foreign policy?

Ethiopia, Gambia, Guinea, Guinea-Bissau.

Technicians of the Watched.

However, I am practicing walking the walk.

"An erogenous zone the size of an index card."

Nice "unique moment" you have there.

"Mr. Z, etc., etc."

I consider myself too young to be reamed in that way.

Soft tissues in three languages.

Unscreened blood, screened shoes.

The problem has not been me, but my inability to admit that I am the problem.

Junkie bike economy.

Having a "past life" only illuminates the library, among the stacks and recalls.

I aspire to a dental plan—to make myself human.

1984: 1.2948.

Rank your unhappiness and then write a book.

"My complex memories of my father are vividly colored by my recollection of Pall Malls, Heaven Hill bourbon and bright red Alfa Romeo Guilietta, take away any of these elements and substitute Kents, champagne or a Pontiac, and I'd be remembering a different man."

Loss is the pleasure of the sexualized sign.

I'm not trying to perceive the world but lozenge senses with a stroke.

Haiti, Kiribati, Lao People's Democratic Republic, Lesotho.

The cultural plan has me a highrise whereas I want to be a stadium.

Guarded argued.

The cold humanizes the city—its body steams.

Is the reverse of moral masochism a military intervention—only the UN's psychoanalyst knows for sure.

Waiting for the train, I'm thinking of you in italics, where the text meets the latex.

So would you like to, uh, ethnography.

An embarrassingly heterosexual reaction to the car.

Do you put apostrophes on yourself—I'm in quotes.

The big trip to Safeway [Canadian reference] today (timeless literature).

The sunlight, idealistic, "cheerful," and unrelenting.

At the moment of address I forget you are dead.

"We're gonna find [a poetics of] feeling good and we're gonna stay there as long as we think we should."

An insomniac's muted blue logo light at ten storeys.

This migraine enables me to view the world anew, pronounced "eyes."

The day, indecisive, disperses.

A class anxiety attack has me destitute after taxes.

1986: 1.3652.

If "workers are those who are not allowed to transform the space/time allotted them," then "takes a licking but keeps on ticking" is a class prospect.

You have to include a little agony in the agony.

Am I *a priori* to you or am I *a priori* to me?

Translatable body language of "I am a prick."

Technicians of the Belatedly Underdeveloped.

Liberia, Madagascar, Malawi, Maldives.

I'm not sure if this syntax lets me "engage" with the world.

"Friends as Footnotes," therefore enemies as endnotes.

This deferral of the day loses the sign or site underhand.

"I've noticed that the tip of my thumb reaches the bottom of some of my suit jackets but not others: How long should a suit jacket be?"

Citizens reproduce themselves.

I'd rather shrink than multiply.

"Arguments opposed: The MLA should not tell people what to do."

I heart carbohydrates.

Weather fulfills the phatic function of language.

"Currently" is proof that ideology is eternal, I'm writing this on February 24, 1995, and you may read it at any following time.

Yell, listen to really loud music, then go out.

Suddenly, cigars: books bigger than my jacket pocket.

Large seventies glasses, like televisions for your face.

A lifetime supply of guitar power chords.

1988: 1.2309.

Made in the image of your workplace, in place of "work," a labour harbour.

Can one holiday without employment?

"Confrontation, Informative: Can you say the same about your phone bill?"

Invertebrate as a corporate logo.

Genre concerns—don't lose my place.

In my lifetime I have witnessed the invention of the Self-Serve Gas Station.

Petrochemically yours.

A non-stet moment developing out of the ether of the day.

Mali, Mauritania, Mozambique, Myanmar.

Between crisis, been in the verb of immigration as DNA.

A petit me epistemology.

Why fronts.

"Thus the interest in faeces is continued partly as interest in money .... "

1990: 1.1668.

A phrase or utterance stripped of its context as a timeless device?

A slough of pop culture with its eternal returns.

Monopolistic tendencies, then the highest stage.

"I have three pairs of clip-on suspenders which I wear frequently with my business suits ... I need to know if these suspenders are considered fashionable."

Every day is Male Pride Day.

Polyphonic saturated thoughts—footnote the music.

You don't need me to tell you this.

"As a banker or a citizen."

I'm so bored with the ATM.

The Buzzcocks are ideology under three minutes.

Nepal, Niger, Rwanda, Samoa.

It's only in the process of writing that we notice this, for your comments please phone 1-800-ask-jeff.

I own markings—make mine gelatin.

"Save As" goodbye finger labour.

If the city is sexualized, then the landscape is screwed.

Is there a psychology of the oppressor?

"White Rastas back to Africa."

Technicians of the Technical.

1992: 1.2083.

The Canadian Prime Minister quotes Popeye on identity.

"I've got your stomach thing."

São Tome and Principe, Sierra Leone, Solomon Islands, Somalia.

The unimaginable conversation outside of commerce.

I want an Art more complicated than The Gap.

Don't Lunacharsky me.

"Take me in your arms / And ameliorate me baby."

Social facts are vertical.

"Before October, Formalism was a vegetable in season."

Please tell the government to stop sending me cheques.

Momma, take my adrenal glands, I don't need them anymore.

It wasn't that you hated me, but everything about me.

Sudan, Togo, Tuvalu, Uganda.

Self-censorship—rarely practised by the right people.

A liberal reaction of the embarrassed subjectivity.

"Opoyaz is the best teacher for our young proletariat writers."

1994: 1.3659.

"You're looking at one Canadian—he's got pressures."

The aliens were gentle, but did not offer me a permanent position.

Or just thanks for the hostility.

United Republic of Tanzania, Vanuatu, Yemen, and Zambia.

The 48 least.

When one's minimums are not being met.

"U.S. dollar in Canadian dollars, average noon spot rate."

"It's odd that their quest for justice has led the various regulators and prosecutors to big Wall Street firms."

Is all space scaffolding?

Expansion.

Nobody Likes You

If the universe
(and I'd include you in it)
is structured as a language
then life is like
being read aloud to. This history, this
series of small crises
that extended form
an epoch that's pocked
with the "news
of the day" contains
contradictions comfortably.
[Devices. Arise.] But I've
become blank
and locked, a bank
back to gold in nervous times
that cloud my value. My original
reasons are gone—keep it
that way, sway or fold
under (blunder) when the questions
come in. Is it all just working
out of how one's family
went from Woolco to Zellers
and then finally, ultimately
without a choice transnationally
to Wal-Mart
as one's way of life
became more and more static

as culture as a whole shut down
every option that one
could have imagined but now
can't even do that? [Economic.
Flexibility.] Cars pass, the farm
is up for sale
but we followed capital
into the city
to populate its edges, producing
paper, communications
thinking that we were making
decisions. Dear unnamed placeless Empire
directly over us
take it easy, eh. The nation-state
is your friend and we
all live in them
more or less. Then the pathetic
teenage years I here
now share with you; the music
the moves the fledgling lingering
lingeries hung heavy with
the sexualized torpor
of ropes, that ropey way
of loping arms and legs
on loan. But the post-war brocade
is carpeted over now
with a value-added
cover version of "American
Woman." An intense
hatred or deep, what, desire
to spit on the man who

shopped by crossing
the picket line but he'd
surely beat the shit
out of me. Under conditions
of my own making. These low-level
returns as actions
of products not of
people (formerly "things"). Killing me softly
with your architecture.
Affronted with
the force of firmness.
Don't go, return
as farce. [Ethical. Investment.] Touch
tempted information mimics
a technology where materials
drape screens on building
façades; it's a boom
and bust experience
(are you?). There is space
but I can't say that
it's social. Danish
modern second hand. Canada
I like it, but I don't know
if I could make a living there.
[Cultural. Heritage.] They are
"Poles" because
they came here, because
they were invested in
or clothed as farmers, former
living hunkies. The streets
are unpeopled

except for servicemen
servicing the seemingly empty
houses (as the camera pulls
back to a crane shot
of the architectural logic). The clouds
are cleaner. A tag or tug
that underbites, that's the tow
of entitlement. It's the urban experience
without the urban! Inverse
on the class scale (psychological
if). I'm cooling my core
as one's habits, or habitus
that led me here. [Policy. Makers.]
Workers cross their own picket line
surely a lifetime supply
of employee of the month
photos there. *Embedded elegy.*
People live and die here
snowboarding out of bounds
this makes it a place
although the logic
is late. A bad day
in the world system
rubs out tempted warnings, I'm
here as milk
on a lip. Then the sun
bounces off the ground's
property. Pull out the porn
for the sliding selection, an uncanny
moment of better breathing. The opening
guitar chords of I feel hot

I feel fucked up and can't be more
definitive than that with a tuck in
fold or sweeping gesture
of please care. It's carnal
carpal tunnel, for like mink
make mine milky
and I appreciate your distanced
fevers flocked to my flesh
barbed blankets chorus. [Development. Goal.]
The Driver, to himself: What
did you expect, asshole
when you make decisions
only for yourself? Applause
or worse, understanding and
a Kruder Dorfmeister remix album
(now passé!) of your past tunes? It's precisely pricks
like you that give
pricks a bad name. So go fuck
off internationally like others could
give a shit. I hope your stereo
breaks down and you get loads
of parking tickets until
you understand what you've done
fucking people's lives. Now, sure
go write it down sympathetically.
Every two hours, this turn of typos
relegating real relations to an
emotion that's a cold cusp
where were you when. [International. Community.]
Patched in and up for smashed
adjacent admiration, how to act

when the hollowness hits, when
it hits hard. Lastly two
dollars rub together in a primacy
collecting covert hedged touches
under dim-lit tables, how can I mistake
this for any other utterance
than utter utility (use value
rules!). As if nightly
my kidneys were to burst
with the joy of clear alcohol
a birthright sought in the soil
of east meets west and an inheritance
of swamp. Worse, what's
such a ribbed tenderness necessity
of warmer targets, for that
knees on lorazepan. I hear the drumsticks
tapped together overhead
so let's start something new
for three and a half minutes
and make it erotic questions
gruffer than the goodness of RPM
on the dial dear. How's it to endure
when angry bitten elbow to the head
model of talking it out shoots
into one's bloodstream, like reams
of reaming twice to the temple
and hope to sleep. [International. Trade.]
Holidays of overtime
come down the line. Popular (populus)
places pass without design
where I'm moody handling

sharps. Back before there was
graphic design, when modules
were easy tangle-free
fetching of public body parts
and lovely elated
modes of production prevailed
you were my favourite
thing. Bourgeois barricades
stop the attack on
adolescence, loosen the thot
police thumb screws
of the redesigned Volkswagen
Beetle, exclamation point.
But forgiven, there's room
for hatred to reside or
ride the misanthrope public
transit. [Poverty. Reduction.] World weary
wanderers let me live a life
of sex and fifty-per-cent taxes
enhanced by other
peoples' lives
(and I'd include yours in it)
which go missing into the vanishing point
driving a seventy-two
white Dodge Charger
ported and polished hemi. Dumping
point of all "negative
thoughts" (not "capability"!) extended
into sentences
that are a technology
as paper and the railroad

once were: is geography
all accumulation
or passive temporal communication (Nokia, Keanu).
Is technology the uncle
of oppression or the
collage method of the gods? Moving through
the external world (*foco* theory: socialism
in one pocket)
on a false passport
with the wrong hair colour
looking for safe cells
in the rental market of Sunset Park's
up & coming. Remember revolutions
happen or are made depending
on which side of the Sino-Soviet split
you fall to (recall the Congo). Large lawn
darts as ethnic in-joke. It's more
than ice pick versus suit
but driver versus passenger
if history is the car. [Relevant. Stakeholders.]
An air index warning or NASDAQ disaster
for you is so dotcom commerce that sounds
surf the sluice but
hounds the master. Pet sounds. Advertising
zeppelins, leaden in the haze
of Indy Weekend. I once had a job
or should I say
it once had me. Touch
my pylon and you play
with fire sir. Rude, infantile
uncommunicative, selfish

(self-centred), worried about loss
of control, why be rude, why
treat people so
poorly, why inflict your mood
on everyone? Suddenly, the world so filled
with possibility as small under-urban
moments or soothing hampers
and aesthetic below-the-belt twitches
teach us how to live with the clean
surfaces of events and ample seasonal
goods. I'm slaw, it slays me. [Fostering. Transparency.]
I'm cooped for the coming crash
of Cronenberg stocks: dots
and loops repeated. Places
to know Wichita lineman. A leak (teak) at
the oil pressure sensor of
my collected or selected
post-war divide of the world
acceleration tapering
now into this fiscal structure
of feelings. Days, these. Don't
those. [Sustainable. Development.]
Report on business. Report on
culture. Don't play
"economic Darwinism" to my nature
despite the gauze wraps
of weakness expounded (Pound!)
from my quarter. Thursday leads
to a pessimism Friday
that is hard to walk through
to a general anger irritate

Saturday. Bad patch. At moments
of access, class collisions on
spec tacked to ethics of asthma
and a zealless self. [Debt. Reduction.]
A controlled narcissism sometimes simply
drifts through a soft-rock afternoon
as experiences that you
don't have access to (again!) are elitist
even if it's down on the machinist's floor.
World info pact parked in Sweden
than wine. But people, call them
friends, behind the short waves
want that timeless effect
in which style is a subtle
mod or teddy boy acting on
determinants as articulated sta-press.
Mental note (metal)
try to be friendlier (international
moments), try to make
friends, try not to be mean
in the morning. As a ream
of sovereign subjects
set up their own web
sites (sorry *hombresito*, Blogs!). Days like this
I ask myself, why can't it be all
snowboarding all the time
with stylish oversized hi-tech clothing
instead of minor misery
on the outskirts of gated communities
with their own flags. The warmth of vinyl
as I "walk from café to bar"

with the psychic life of pronouns
against a shitty nationalism
that makes me
internally bourgeois with a budget
"restless and bored" waiting
for the Bill Wither's electric piano
vibe to set us free. Huh? Will you be my
John Kenneth Galbraith? [Capacity. Constraint.]
Couples in same clothing will line up
for a restaurant, artisanal bread, organic
coffee, but not for you. I guess
that's love outside
of a linguistic experience
and into a discursive curve
of North American fun
consumption as radical liminal
acts: so, look good
smash the state and give us
a call, we're available. Please stop
me from rewriting the *Iliad* Dad
because I always got car sick
in my mirror stage
despite the symbolic
highway. [Market. Access.]
Route One (sing the song)
because it is the only one:
to this am I
now saying goodbye
cultural nationalism
as kitsch (hey check out
my puck collection!) and nomadic hipster

lifestyle (*ID*, *The Face*, *Harvard
Design Magazine*, Frank O'Hara, etc.) gone speculative
transnational, that's the question. Eat
my recipe! Eat the rich?
The Driver to the Passengers: So
you think you've been fucked over
but it's otherwise. This is the one time
that I am right. Here's some advice:
Blame yourselves. Do you want me to say
what people really say
about you, do you
want me to say that? Even if I am fucked
in the head, you are too
so you can get out of the car
and—as we say where I'm from
and not the planet you
live on—shut up and put up. So, go
get back to your lives
that would bore even
a stick shitless.
(Word is fast saving Nobody).
World minutes for unseen forces
that, to quote the man (murderer?)
in the pajamas, "perceived-
accepted-suffered." That said, join
us on the buffed birch
floor so we can wriggle
a little something, something. The Kris
Kristofferson of cultural
studies, the ambient dub
of postcolonial theory, the Domino

Theory of the open text. "Sir, or
Squire, do not be so
'Happy Sad,' it doth not
befit you in today's marketplace
of poetics as unfinished
class war: instead assert
your imperial view
from here." [Performance.
Benchmarks.] So, when you say "Eat
the rich" it's not so much a speech act
but an iterative position?
It is the tyranny of "Casual Fridays"
I speak of, this afternoon
with global capitalism
stretching out
time. [Heightened.
Uncertainties.]

Forced Thoughts

perceived accepted suffered
merely naturally unites
veils cultures call
time annihilates space

jobbers thoughts press
lobes I've always
valves wavered lost
parasite pure person

federal pattern of
feral worker free
family the state
that is whose

ethnic bad body
allegory product of
levels sleeve verve
connectivity amidst city

deep faux fur
fetish city suckle
little loud inside
cosmopolitanism chalks bread

cost of doing
just fucked flexi
my new melancholy
an historical descent

alumni bell curve
the states illegal
capitalists border faults
plural art ruralified

amongst pods gone
multi utopia people
look up at
geopolitics in aluminum

service industry loop
this little light
purpose dry immigrant
the drier the

culture structure of
happy hour allowed
right of centre
when centre is

market flood for
mystery scare imagine
said deeds substitute
written for distribution

previous employment loyalty
like this deeper
brighter days pushing
time to scale

rebate before blow
cyborgs everything your
yesterday sturdy study
lefty talk radio

pressure drop during
gag reflex on
meet the press
heritage vernacular accident

ruin bitter men
for lack bricoleur
burnt sad cohesive
it's a colour

neighbourhood mosh pit
in a magazine
indexed purple hunch
run length fully

flippy full flexes
photos inhabited tidal
thigh wavy anyway
indexical architecture angle

good knob heaven
holy crap reaper
for those about
wobble middle ground

mind map howdy
triple hiatus word
embrace the bigness
that business blossoms

in its own
image of accumulation
latte mutation age
all because of

purge tell let's
everyone sperm ahoy
industry in literature
truth in work

bolt run-away factories
noun canada noun
unity inuit vote
my emergent numbness

a little limp
slide support post
cut life stripes
hospitals were workers

historically variable minimum
minder torch touch
education sip structure
day little me

het the mal
room abnormal malice
drift absolute tour
first yes saves

so you uncle
perfect for flat
four or number
to entries race

wet the start
for face velvet
long false veil
miniature kitchen eames

diplomacy velvet value
vanguardist so called
social everyday very
consciousness dot dot

no more two
word titles dethrone
friesland or fleck
france petite boycott

parental pressure point
tighter and tighter
that cultures us
spot marks spot

late sexualized imagery
blurry yet rumoured
impatient told me
hold that thing

articulation not representation
deep military experience
suck a calendar
time us up

gimme program doing
it big time
I forget the
numbers bathed in

headbanger t-shirt collection
his election to
lose whatever horde
pissed people off

extant historical conditions
everywhere lowered blinds
expectations respects ready
made state machinery

immaturity stripped bookstore
vapour lock then
the house painter
total hard core

obligation to plagiarize
spontaneist diamat headgear
the gap outfit
helping keep kelp

lets terrytowel again
toward a low-flying
jet enjambment office
too cubicle class

enemy "poems" suddenly
deep happy irony
hegemony dentist arts
the song now

furious middle practice
gingham expansion european
indigenize personal pronoun
numbs big job

application plies lesions
hernia hopeful opal
cadet brussels common
couth sought mouth

double oppression mint
flavour polar fleece
production for need
avoid work week

no way means
button-down classless society
nights for which
night goes blank

I seek psychology
early modern mennonites
advance package advantage
attractive and justificatory

lyric lycra crawls
to be with
people plus us
cars need youth

how much dutch
gilds golden lode
sex walk tie-in
bookish acquaintance repetitive

stress syndrome series
pre-genital phases sets
seventies mop-up recession
empire practices campus

radical demonstration dispersal
sallow crowd counts
an entire empire
periphery versus city

flow of labour
low of our
six figure fellows
style double style

the twelve words
of me menial
epics some snaps
at hemp helm

nervous city space
all day generals
same day initials
slant six rev

general bodily arousal
human adrenal gland
this foreign three
chord progression captain

into the worst
architecture blocks of
lack dampened it
got wet right

some facts for
all tax cut
revision of my
retooled toil frisk

at an age
where fiscal feign
I'll alleviate all
whimper to wet

or available compass
twist on fine
iron blank ballast
ways to go

twelve book format
chip away days
in a gauge
support the economy

THE HIGHEST STAGE

Take this, then, as the question
whether "what we share"
is stasis or place

where small, immobile
mappings bore (bare) their scale
the city's

edges aerosol patterns
of living
a hard history

on a loop. Soft as money
in a mattress
those intimate moments

await reclamation (squandered
generations), primitive, piled
and petrol. It's a cruel

landscape escapade to earn
the a) accumulation strategy b) buoyant
life c) scarcity since it is

capitalism's intimate moments
that address countries
as individuals

and vice versa. The cities are
a strip crisis clustered
to the south. The car

is a machine of relations. I know
and am driven by this. As if
this is a reply

to produce you. Today
I thought to add "My life
is miserable, June 25, 1996"

but I'd have to believe
a) that b) moments
not spaces c) there

are potential
audiences for such
extended solos.

"I wanted his
head" the intruder said
and this specificity

is hard not to admire. So
how do I live
with myself? In the seventies

Chile was an international
image and now if "make the economy
scream" was Nixon's wish

then countries are humans
and I want to deflect
this "eternally."

Live in this city
and live longer
unfortunately.

Central [Canada] Party Haus

For a street

Localism robs us
of our history. Cities
are quantity
taken qualitatively. Your shirt
is a living example
of the alienation of labour.
The problem of pronouns
per pound. Andy
works the Cameron
on Monday nights. The Gap
just across the tracks
shows how the forces
of NATO and NAFTA have made
it easy to look good casually.
Is this personism
in a world-class city [only Regina
exempts itself] or canon reformation
suitable for public transit? Did I
mention the Arts? The society of the
ever-deepening who-
dunnit. The lush life is ripe
on the corner. Martha
Stewart's Productivist dream
realized through Zellers (dented
by insider trading).
Gardening is the opiate
of the bourgeoisie! Belated Canadian modernism

is pressure-molded plastic! Sure it's easy
to be critical, but try
looking good doing it! Mussolini
wore khakis. George C. Scott as Patton
wore khakis. The lack of a unified address
["Tansy buttons, tansy / for my city … " etc.]
makes me a symptom: cognitive mapping
for the spatially spaced. Yes, yes
Hockey Hall of Fame. I'm specific, I'm
particular platinum at
a pronounced pace: one
can only negotiate
these contradictions textually
or risk a president's choice
kneecapping in an ample
parking lot. Local! Sub-local!
Suburban dog attacks followed
by children falling from balconies.
And it's just like Earle Birney said
to Leon Trotsky: a) "It's been a great
party" b) "Historically,
we're screwed" c) "After that it was
fashionable / for a time to be internationable."
But now the rain falls straight
and people in other cities
have natural and rational
economic nervousness bloated globally.
Maximus to Hogtown? I think I prefer
the residue of The Rex. "An [citizen]
is a complex of occasions" … compelled
to bigger and better speech
acts of polis and spoil.

Social Facts Are Vertical

It's not often I lament a product.

I'm 162 years younger than the term *ideology*.

People bloom.

"We 'persons' therefore are artifacts of labour" or fluctuating wages.

The homes on display are not display homes.

This film is "historically accurate."

"What is important, however, is not to be a Monday morning quarterback to the world's antisystemic movements."

Sucking the pleasure right out of it breaking the trademark.

Tokyo, Tokyo, Tokyo.

Mood of production: through what do I decipher myself.

I am the same age as the term *ugly American*.

Capitalism, no longer able to be embarrassed, it's not "all so beautiful …. "

Overcomes strong feelings by not caring (world system).

Boil It Off the Bone: The Collected Poems.

Does desire deepen or disperse when sleep steps in.

The sky sweeps by—this is coverage at its finest: the landscape is value to happen.

I have an idea of me (I have ID).

An individual, say person, history rounded deft surface course.

New York, New York, Mexico City.

Being naked in another language or at least appearing so.

Canadian signage of traveling—what's the story (morning sickness).

"A pathology of atmosphere."

The sex commercials made me drink the water (bubbly subtext).

Smoking, not as easy as the industry would have you believe.

This city needs a rain; a hard rain in a sleepy town.

The cars outside are singing, that's the rights that won't be shimmied.

"Thus history replies, 'Who will do the dirty work' .... "

And who remembers the Squamish Five?

This one's going out to my detractors out there in their tractor caps (class solidarity).

A day of similes (smiles) finally.

A personal moral (mole) outrage applied to friends at a distance: that's a big ten four or "fuck you very much."

Can we blame it on the discovery of the double-entry bookkeeping system?—I doubt it.

Mexico City, Mexico City, Bombay.

"This applies to everything you purchase."

We just wanted to hear ourselves say it.

Suddenly nausea, and it's not just transnational.

Like a jury (for the very first time).

Will you do what hasn't been done to me?

"How to identify a worker"—they're the ones on display.

Velvet Revolution balcony bullet holes of the closest reading of architecture.

"I am also postponing, for a short time, the exposition of my analysis of anxiety."

What, the Human Conditioner?

The back-lane bottle economy on wobbly bikes in a centreless city.

São Paulo, São Paulo, São Paulo.

Please enter my mode of production, momentary and mummified like a lock is to logic.

Is pleasure use value you can't cash in? (farewell eighties!)

"A similar tendency can be seen with underwear, shoes, basic furniture, etc.—at least in the richest countries."

Scientific, like aviator glasses.

"Target as small as an arm or a leg."

Thirty thousand dollars of untaxed corporate profits a minute in Canada: don't forget to personalize the "national" "debt."

"How are we going to see those who we have not yet seen"—by asking them to appear differently.

Piano from a houseboat.

Between the "discursive" and the "event" … there has to be something worth photographing.

Glands against classism.

Shanghai, Shanghai, New York.

"Bathed in money."

You are value waiting to happen.

So, in order to vote you have to ask yourself are you any better off since you began reading this poem or has your economic situation remained the same?

Hey, that's my ashtray collection.

"Safety, marksmanship, judgment, dynamic situation simulation."

Does your sculpture just stand there, or does it spin?

You make me feel like having my own "internal crisis."

Imagine yourself a geopolitical power, imagine me at your side.

"The problem of getting workers to work harder for lower pay is inherently difficult."

If "the workingmen [sic] have no country" then there can be no working-class nationalism: how does this explain hockey?

Osaka, Bombay, Lagos.

"Let us look more closely at these three relations [At this point the first manuscript breaks off unfinished]."

I questioned authority and the question won.

Once your ethnicity is reduced to cooking, it's a lot easier to join the parade.

Can you parody something you are a part of?

It's "cult of facts" time again.

Suited to the "suppressed actualities" you see in others but imagine your own.

"In North America, it's very important not to confuse consumers."

"Thematically a book like P. Inman's *Uneven Development* is impossible to corral semantically even uneven development as the form globalization takes in the world": I wrote.

The quotation marks from one word, like a performative middle-aged biker on holiday.

The randomness was as ice.

Buenos Aires, Los Angeles, Los Angeles.

Before I understood moods.

The linebreak possibilities of "I feel funny."

Is it unreasonable to think that I am reasonable and you are not?

His card simply read "expert."

And it is from here that my small yet "stylish" life emanates (or, hey man what did we ever do to you?)

Melt-down sentimentality for new technological changes in long-distance rates, I'd like to be tied down for the majority of the afternoon.

World of flows filled with foes and woes.

Ideas will do.

And I do.

The practice of plastic.

Los Angeles, Buenos Aires, Calcutta.

Is the "middle class" a race?

Is management a culture?

"I dare say that no one else is writing lines such as 'voids convivial handtray intubation' .... "

An oil strong enough for today's hyper-referential poetry.

Cheap suit—I'm impressed.

Haig, what is a Haig—is it like a Swartzkopf?

I see the boys walk by with their sunburnt nose.

I'm barely getting wider.

A hard rain is hail (gonna).

Calcutta, Osaka, Shanghai.

Mind the bollocks.

I missed the "Kiss Me I'm Polish" moment.

Tell your momma and papa that I'm a graduate school boy too.

Momma, seize this mastercard from me, they won't let me use it anymore.

Please mail traced outlines of your body on an 8 ½ x 11 sheet to me at the above address.

So, you are your own source material?

Beijing, Calcutta, Buenos Aires.

If I could be your Tuesday Weld late-fifties photo jangley guitar pop tune then would you butter perfect harm.

I'm smoking dynamite, listening to TNT and reading GQ like never before: I'm ready, ready as any man'll be.

I don't believe that anyone thinks of you sexually as I do after all.

Uh oh autobio.

"This is the modern world," chord, chorus.

At ten cents a word, this poem is worth $109.50 so far.

Don't melt on me, melt with me.

I'm going to have to ask you to be nonsexual now.

I am 43 years older than the term "weapons of mass destruction."

It was only then that "I realized I had repressed something."

Paris, Beijing, Dhaka.

In the "movement from nature to culture," where are you.

"It's human nature to do everything you can to stop the puck from going in the net."

If I were to dedicate this to "The Ruling Class," would that be dated?

Embarking on a critical study of Paul Weller's political sonnets of the Interregnum period.

Hey Cultural Studies, leave those kids alone.

Paradise Lofts.

I think I am a better person than I think I am.

Yuri Gagarin was technology at that point, now he's a space training centre for rent.

The term oral has been recuperated from poetics by personal ads.

Rio de Janeiro, Seoul, Karachi.

"You think that, having planted a kidney bean in a flower pot, you are capable of raising the tree of proletarian literature."

Canadian federal policy on child poverty parallels Michael Jackson.

I am one month older than "Mr. Clean."

Europe, better sweaters, (duffer ethnography).

Stop listen what's that sound of the architects listening to the margins of modernism.

Or the Empire wrote back and said, You got something to say?

The album that saved you during your teenage years.

I'm six years older then the term *gentrification*.

"My car is toast."

Cities Trading Places on the Top 30 List.

Just happy to be here.

"More business."

JOBBER

sweeping compressed
accumulation, dented
decade on any
given Sunday, the real
sham strives
to pension person
not people, stampede
party card carrying
"governmentality" so
many "friendly dictators" away
from the pace, should I
die at home or
should I stay now, Davos
of world literature
workers, petroleum
portfolio packers, and
"endlessly consume
youth", pan
orb compromise
towards such a lot
of crap Mr. Qualitative versus
Sr. Quantitative, each
purchase grips
my home despot
ordeal, rocky
to the right, content
to reach an age, cheat

"diminished"
expectations, hostility to how
in general, my relation
to the classics condensed
through a coil, why sweat
for someone
else, a response
to quelch, dear read
control roll bar
of excess supplement, mine disaster
minute, mutual fund
remembered, plot
blight, at the
holy shit level of
good-evil, so
benign its churned
in butter barrels
of central committees, heritage
for the homeland phonebook, real
or merely illegal
humans (labour), fast density
is urban edge city, an allegory
of ouch stretched
to an epic, nervous
to get local
from the waist up, the horror
of calendars imposed
from above, permissible
and ignored solidarity
lapel pins
with maple leafs, I have tried

to define delimit, it's
a look
a look of
leverage, mountie
in a snowstorm copyright
violation, friendly fire
in the desert
of the willing, design problems
of the panopticon how to
overcome, red minister
of fisheries take a piece of
my cod, a touch
their flukes interactive
display, a dinosaur
economy of oil, they had a
strike and it
worked, job for life
China into the WTO, taken
out of the anthology
in subsequent reprintings, when
text stands in
for perplexed, when lamination
was a technical
innovation, the old
Rome and the new
Empire, the birth
of the person
who fights
for 30-day refund rights, so slow
it's obsolete
as Oslo, more domes (doms)

for mod people, the economy
of alert, at this I'd
side with the logic
of the vapour lock, wake
up and restore
the store to
its glory, such centuries dusted
with pamphlet parliaments
and the attempt
of a flip, call it a coup, clueless
guesses soft subs for community
out of industry, put in
a post, way
that you feel why, help
it, collected memos
of management
teams, but a belated eulogy
for others, over
draft protection
would be safe money
like pulling pupils
from a barrel, can't
help it, I don't
so much want to have
affect but to have
measures, when
was the last
war for a global
citizen before
"flowering of
the rods", this was

your historical failure
written from the inside
tossed aside from
the outside, just
trying to make sense
of the rich folks'
ways, beehive
in architecture, brinksmanship or
high-flying
war-criminal
vacation packages, Tuesday
September 11th 1973, definition
retrograde days, and if
the patterns are me
please purge, all tomorrow's
avant-gardes, Hong Kong
as the analog, murky
it moves to
a them, America's problem
with islands, ownership
responsibilities of the
it's yours but you
don't deserve it, was
there supposed to be
the corresponding
physical effect, hard really
to believe in yourself
a self like silt
or salmon on
a ladder, or new
laddishness, welcome

rotarians, there goes my
vocabulary playing tricks
with my liver again, forced
air, hello walls
hello polyurethane
coated floors, is it
vintage silver lining
lead casing within
industrial standards, adrenal
dump, target
small as an arm
or a leg like a light
swinging from a willow
branch, super store
ethnic aisle, the farmer
farmed, a latin
howdy, suddenly
secular, good dad bad dad
diplomacy, airline thing
I think, "trade irritant"
of nonplaces, suddenly
space for the taking, run
at the cougar Canadians, I could
be where anywhere, North America
hence take-out
coffee, sue me
yes "lofts," yes frontier-making, career
car expectation, I now know
semantic means, like
a stump, sports
deaths, coffee

is the new oil, right worth what
takeover, grapes
are unionized why
not you, it's this
cabbage that is
my baggage, visible
from the sky, heritage
farm heritage home heritage
immigration policy, throttle
in a bottle, plank
for the future, you're so
UNICEF, I'm sorry
I like suede, when
one's life is neutral
like Costa Rica in
a consulate, haunted but
just for men, I'm helping
small business meet
their goals I'm
the Business Development Bank
of Canada, disagree on
the numbers but it
was a *crowd*, down
now businesses "panic"
like encyclopedias, answer the ad
for an MP, slow
sadness, in a show
of support for
the employees the board
quits, absolved, the shoe
gazer ruled, if eating

a banana is imperialism
then is a kiwi
neocolonialism, alienated
from even your
toast or socks, colder
than recycling, recycling
what, the all-donated rice diet
is the special today, these new forms
of governmentality
dropped from friendly
B52s, pharmaceutical samples
best before, bit bad
bite back, street-cred architects
of the wavey
shoe display, new sub
festivities of supply
side logic of late, plateau
to go, I bought
the self-help legal
handbook and won, teeth
just proved impractical
and expensive, exposed skin
just a romantic idea, we named it
after you and we're going to
come calling, the cars
produced themselves
as post-Fordist pods, lament
for a Saskatchewan, just
watch me war measures
again and globally, neither
country nor city

but low cinderblock
buildings, stickers
of my youth
restore to me
the powers
of the basement
bedroom, tighten the pants
of cosmopolitanism, my
vocabulary is unemotional
therefore I am an inferior
model, cloned
gnomes, the guide
to pleasures under
ten dollars, potentials
that I can borrow, like
a leaf on the tree
of tomorrow, the only
bland that matters, interview
with the candidate, remixes
from earlier discs, I only
hoped for a film fest
in your honour
never anything less, that
petrol emotion, getting
ready to have been
detoxified, today's
danger is real and present
and everywhere, no unjust
desires just
mainly marketed hailings
of some simperings

I never had the chance
to "voice" that verb, grueling
cloud cover, smouldering
documented career moves, car
pools, so much
stucco, hate me less
loan me more, extreme
cold weather alert
for the economic underclass, Toronto
the former, at these
prices no wonder, may contain
peanuts, a hostile call
from the census people, ruse
to recall, it's *down* the
computer is *down*, thus they
were bad and deserved
financial ruin, would you
recognize the public
sphere if it came
in a plain brown bag, dukes
of, if you didn't
already notice
we are a collective, trunked
and truncated, family
found house sold
signs, automobiles populate
my city like inhabitants
before profit
was history, self-imposed
exile from working
class, your keychain is happy

to see you, umlaut
of Iron Man, technology
and grieving, the resurgence of
orange and lime
green is the dream
of mass modernism, it's my
head, is to tinker
to dick with, downcast
customers stomach mach
one, the length of the look, the
stretch and fudge
of the press, surplus
workers of the beer
industry we
salute you for our lives
have been enriched
by your former labour, work
at home in your pajamas
because that's agency
and solid single
sucking, can we
OPEC, my head that's what's
killing me, indignant for
decades, but can I
give it if so, design ideas for
the modular creamy
beige outlook with books
for ballast, so scary so
family orientated, the logic of
just one touch just
one touch, at the

cellular level, a word you
would use, could I then
just look, a late
sixties early seventies
euro speed slip, WTKOed, I
phoned for an appointment
against alienation, it's
a big project

"Mao's Gift to Nixon"

Panda. Contradiction. Bonjour
Bon Jovi. Yet the effortlessness
of moving through social space
underground
in a language
orange and grey
better suited to you
(polyvinyl). One-
stop riders disengage
against the false hostess
of transit police! But
the accent
doesn't so much beckon
as reckon.
Dear Jeff, "I'm not
a radical avant-gardist, I
just want
to broaden the concept
of pop music." Dear Brian, when I
say "Hand me the
screwdriver"
I am saying my cultural
heritage counts. When I say "turn the Bon
Jovi up, Jeff," I'm
saying my cultural
heritage should always be
played

at full volume. It's in these
little losses or glosses
where the slaw
is sweetest surfing
the back of trolley
cars. Normative poems
for my friends
deep ends
of volleys from the ballrooms
and secret saunas
where the "downcast eyes"
come with a coversheet. I've meant
to be mean, son, and so on. I've meant
to be my men-
acing metaphysics, but the
vertical colour of sound is
sumped, a tension of obligatory
pleasures, anticipatory
spas-on-hold. "Here I come
to save the
day," that means Mighty
Mouse is synchronic cash. An interview's
afterglow, signs grounded
in confectionery lice. It looks
like it's Friday
the 13th on Easter Island
all over again, Brian, tied
in the umlaut of my love
and the slipstream
of transnational grinder culture's
homosocial ale. Ice, conveniently

neighbour, and our offices
are the street's kino
lacking limos for keynote
speakers. Industry, man, gender
investigative reporters
rogue investors with blue
blood brogues and a toque
for the miserable
Habs. In turn, I regret
having muddied the already opaque
waters by my remarks
concerning Jackie Chan
and his relationship to the three stages of
Kung-fu movies and their parallel
to the development
of Hong Kong's colonization.
Plus the internet. It's so boring!
So incredible. Most
poetry written
in America would not be
if these simple steps.
It's so imploring
to keep importing food
into your body. Hence
the return of the person
the pronoun
of the pizza. Edit
was act but
now it's my unique
subjectivity glittery
amongst the consumer goods

and my fabulous pals
consuming as radical
rearticulatory pleasure and then
Brian, the artist reproduces the cover
of a Flock of Seagulls' album
and the Nair. But mine
is better because the products
I mention are cooler " a carton of Gauloises
and a carton / of Picayune", versus
72 Dodge Challenger, altho
Schuyler is hard to beat
with "The Mod Squad" and a shopping list
with "Lee Riders." Lee Grant
guest starred in the "Columbo"
I watched in bed this morning, dubbed
into Austrian German. (See
how easy it is!) Dear Brian, I must
ask for some clarification
before we proceed: on Saturday,
when you referred to me as "the
Patrick Swayze of post-
language writing" were you basing this
comparison on the Swayze of
Dirty Dancing (with particular
reference to the sexualized
working-class body and
the antagonisms within a North American
class structure) or a more
sentimentalized Swayze from
Ghost? Were you suggesting
that this provides a paradigm for

the trajectory of my writing practice?
"Should I
check or should I
go, now." And I must concede that
you were more accurate in your application
of *Mars Attacks* ("Bugs in the minds
of the candy masses") to your relationship to
language & hegemony
in your textual production
than I was in my confusion surrounding
Star Ship Trooper, a confusion
which expired any thought
to the spectacle of Patrick Swayze
in drag in the American remake of
Priscilla, Queen of the Desert
("Australian for beer")
to which I was referring, Jeff.
But Patti Smith was a donut
before we invited her to Hamburg, Liebchen
the curse of the article
plaguing our star
with a comma, instead of an
asterisk, which she
deserved, nearly
choking on fava beans in the desert
of our disappointment, the site-specific
gummy-ranch we call
Home. Good news!
The Moog is back from the shop.
The Eno setting's tuned up. All negative
homologies drop away

in bad dog barking, and every white
man shits out his
ass, correct? But, as I have
said before, the universal
is just a particular
that's become dominant, then class structure
(Brooklyn) retains
this. Like: This is your shithole
and welcome to it (at least
it's ours). If our
preliminary transcendence
is false, what plagues for the effigies
of the poster boys, Spock?

Jeff Derksen & Brian Kim Stefans
Brooklyn 2000

"What to Do about Globalism"

People, the. Do I have to do
everything?
Here's how it goes:
Born Work Broken and
Die. That's why
there is such love
in seventies guitar solos.
Kiss your torpor good morning
or goodbye. Learn to fight back against
your foes or the flows of those
global scapes and engines
of enterprise. When good times
get better, when "built space"
is inflatable and clients are giants
of trickle-down taste. From agitprop to diamat
I believe it was Tatlin
who said—or was it Jacques Villeneuve:
Learn to make leisure
more work, rumours over tumours,
strategies over tactics. I stand
before you asking to be memorable
for my memorabilia and
symptomatic for my mottos
in these times when we are told
that movement is what we all share
it's just that some have more legroom.
So when the robots come knockin

for your paper shredder and your lemon juicer
it will not be Jimmy Page or Jimmy Carter
who saves you
but the bright backlit unmitigated moments
of critical art projections that awaken you
to new spatial possibilities right there
in your globally defined local or glaucoma.
"Went on a little walk downtown
where the global hits the local
sweetest thing daddy has ever seen
to bring it on home
in the back of a pick-up
yeah, bring it on home."
And to disrupt rather
than just put up, to puke
than rut. Smart guy is appalled by their
aesthetic choices as people
of the former east block (bloc/bloke)
load furniture into trailers
to tow home. I'm resisting
selling this as "freedom
from exchange" ("even
if it is against his will"). In an international
heaven, you will be mine
with bees buzzing around
the honey pot of collectivity. The wind
in Wien. The rain
in Wancouver, the onions of Walla
Walla are all specifics which should save
us (cast down oh cast
down the satellite dish). Strong

nation-state weak nation-state
arguments versus "global footlooseness
of corporate capital" breaks
the high-school dancing ban. Mired
in the past (method)
buttery soft social state. Imagine, newly
capitalist! Hey the (telos) of modernism
etc. with all this hunched up
crawling after daddy's lawyer
and the petty threats. I don't have
any dot com stocks
so shut up (or market
defeatism). Imagine as if all of it
were attached by a string and that
it made a picture which
was known as folk art. Be kind
to your cat, love
the animals as you cannot love
yourself (yet another reason
for labour unions). Representation, the rest
is just taste tarted up
as cake (former Hapsburg heart buried
in mystery area of Austria). How long
were you planning on sticking
with the two-party system? I read better
in sans serif now that I'm at
the contractual obligation age. Was it
the Canadianization of Brazil
or the Brazilianization of the International Style
that's made an itchy little
trade war, my darling, mein Liebling, mi

vida? (Prada beat America
on water.) The title is a cynical
maneuver to show up on
topic searches and not a manual
for action, so I will not be responsible
for any injuries incurred
(so far there is one
strategy and it's litigious). Fanning the flames
of post-Steve McQueen "modern agents"—put simply
is to recognize what communities are
before we ask them to follow us.
South, naturally, is where
the satellite dishes
connect. Hey man, Ya Basta!
from Prague to Penticton. "Drunkenness
and cruelty." It's a bad day for us
a bad day aesthetically
because we are hosers and not
"stars of track and field"
and now it's time (digital) to
take over overtly tactical. It'd be good
to live in the city
rather than have it
inflicted on you
spatially. Oh, funny
in the face
of *flows*, secondary global currencies.
Average time up from twenty
minutes to three hours defines
"social reproduction." Never before
have I been

so nervous. The constant hum
of low-level nonunion
construction. I changed
your reading practices, now go
change the world son, mussed my
hair and I'm off on my mod
grandpa's Vespa. Like Iceland
he's hot inside, cold outside. What
was the global-local
(Lagos in SoHo) and why
did the phone companies
tell us to organize on
that scale? An itch to one
is an irritant to all or gone
are the jumbo themes we
were weaned on? Good golly
new oligarchy, that's the magic
of The Mall of America
explained like this:
"building for the future"
with pain today. There's the noun
where's the now.

COMPRESSION

"No photos, it's not Disneyland."

Get your avant-gardist good life out of my face!

I'm six years older than the term *gentrification*.

Your "essential historical feature" has been flexibility:
Who are you?

"We should not be embarrassed about our supremacy,
but we should recognize that power alone is not
sufficient to achieve our goals."

A book whose sole index entry under *U* is "Utopia."

"We are better at dropping bombs than we are at
designing a political, cultural campaign."

I was wondering, for this idea of "the political
approach to leisure," if I would have to leave the
house for it?

"'I'm not interested in the rug as a passive thing that
just sits on the floor to make a room more pleasant or
delineate a space.'"

Suddenly a city saturated with police, globally guarding Starbucks.

The narrative that begins, "Under the old capitalism .... "

Insignia remembers.

Canada 581.

Flipside dystopia.

And then opens a hair salon called "Perm Revolution."

The "informal economy" is from other countries; they have people!

Did we internet vote on the name of the First Family's cat, or was it the dog?

I personally have not noticed any new forms of imperialism where I do my shopping.

More chicken than you've ever seen.

A shredded corporation "fights for its life" by laying off 25% of its workers.

"Unless we are maniacally dumb, we are going to win this war; this is an overmatch greater than Desert Storm."

Saudi Arabia 464.

Does this mean we will have to boycott boy bands or can we subscribe on-line?

Like a teddy bear from a catapult, like super-sized pepper spray, like historical necessity behind the wheel of a '68 Camaro.

Unilateral with emphasis on *uni*.

I'm forty years older than the term "contemporary globalized multicultural postfordist metropolis."

"Being freer" or free beer.

Does this mean we will have to firebomb Ikea?

And then it happens in The Netherlands!

An Informalist.

Today the climate is ... "favourable for business."

Pace University remembers.

Mexico 457.

I'd like to join the boycott, but I've internalized everything.

"Everywhere in retreat .... "

Two types of freedom (now seems even excessive).

"For those who embrace the free flow of goods and services around the world, these are disquieting times."

He talks! Stocks drop!

"Skateboarders are litigious businessmen …! "

American casualness (Dock Dock, Clash City Dockers!).

Above your station—the puck!—here it comes now.

Venezuela 433.

I'd like to join the protest, but I don't enjoy having my irises screened.

I'd like to inflate a bubble building as a mobile public sphere, but I'm a little breathless.

I'd like to break the plate-glass windows of globalization, but I need a coffee first.

I'd like to engage in some collectivity, but I'm busy accumulating particularities.

I'd like to "buy the world a coke," but I'm more into critical regionalism than universal civilization.

How can you argue against "pleasure"?: With one arm!

"The President is offended and he thinks that [corporate wrongdoing] does damage to the reputation of a capitalist system which deserves to have a good reputation."

Paper not people!

People not square-footage!

Nigeria 180.

Maniacally dumb!

I'm more nervous than 1973.

I'm a mean man of means by no means.

And they thought "World Music" was imperialism!

Like food from a B52.

Sandler O'Neil & Partners remembers.

The stockmarket is edgy, but you are cool under pressure: who are you?

"So what is the proper etiquette when friends and acquaintances are dragged into scandal?"

Britain 141.

Bank of America remembers.

I'm 32 years older than the term *degentrification*.

Commodification of everything, again.

This makes "primitive accumulation" look like a corporate softball tournament!

Skateboard harder to change the world!

In the global city, 3.2 minutes of "world news" a day.

My mind is alive with the sound of autumnal leaf blowers.

It's a car-care culture.

If commodities could talk, would they walk the walk or balk the hawks?

Iraq 139.

"The rest of the world."

In its own image.

Let everything annoy you.

If "certainty is an expensive luxury," then that means someone can buy it.

"Pinochet Checks Into Hospital," Kissinger still at large.

Brownstone cowboys.

Norway 119.

Do you feel as if you are watching a movie or trying out for a part in the movie?

K-Mart will never forget.

Daddy was a papermaker, but he never pulped nobody, Daddy was a duct-taper but he never duct nobody, Daddy was an investment advisor but he never hurt nobody … etc.

"Did the President tell you something new?"

"I am a carbohydrate person" (later challenged on the talk-show circuit).

He'd drill your ass for oil if he thought it'd get a drop!

"Spending discipline."

I fell asleep on the subway—"Did your shoes get stolen?"

Not nuts enough!

Angola 97.

"Everyone wants shorter flash-to-bang time …. "

The narrative that begins … "When the markets were rising and everyone was getting rich …. "

AON remembers.

"And who will dare cry in the face of all of this— Formalism!"

If capitalism kills you, who do you complain to?

Rock, as in Rock On.

" … at least 30 million PowerPoint presentations are delivered every day around the world."

I'm one year older than "The Kitchen Debate."

(Mississippi Wal-Mart.)

Algeria 84.

The snow is expensive.

Millions of barrels.

As Something Alien

Urban Experience
(Or, "Our Favourite Shop")
for Calgary

Don't make the mistake of mine
imagining moments as systems
it's death in a dial
why theory sings for
poorly made mystified calls
on the street to turn to
from the designers of
"punitive and reduced"
how the caucus split
comes into your life
despite supreme court bulldozers
pushing equality
that French thing
into your back forty
hail alleviate local unearthly Stalin's
corporate counterpart punctures
if you're human
humanism is a nice promise
glows grey then against
homosexual education package
need you ask
smoke my windows
how hollow inside in
such a personal religious holiday

Okotoks Ottakring in the creeping
"creepiness" of culture
there needs to be water
turned into vodka (rough
translation) to even live today
I think of you
locally globally "glocally"
small screen subverts this very
vocabulary for more Vienna
synth-pop social spaces
for reading and sitting
history, a condition of
just what part of fuck you
did you not internalize
I love the music's
sleek suit of censorship
and spine's mortal joy machine
an exuberance of tan and brown
in an environment of grind
outside the bad history of
me, that capitalist innovation
leaks into this wobbly present
out of moods a wood
resides in thinking
three metres of comfort
all I ever drove down
highways of garnisheed direct deposits
and aesthetics that I can't use
if only the pivot
were volatile or votive
toiling voters

Space Replaced (Over Time)

for Vancouver

A time when spaces
opened as voices
and seeing yourself meant
handles dealt with real
modernist unmaskings of power
using glass passively
exaggerated places
felt reflectively
strange now (really) speculative
in an isolation of aggression (secession)
and vibrant "youth cultures"
condensed into scents
that there never was
any resistance here
just a history of how
much I think
I hate it now
nervously waking
in older dead lives
piled into sodden republic
dumpsters as distribution deals
midway woods with moods
making a larger shard
harder than even
those little linked moments *(Uberblik)*
that make up the past
dealt as the eighties

and all the lovely formative
checks (cheques) the tiny
scams the cabs the pubs
the discoveries of parts
of the port city that now are long
articulated into "the failure
of social housing" (rotting condos)
versus Karl Marx Hof
and the textual joke of "glocal"
would have then the styles
that seem determined and gooey
in comparison sombre
with the docks being a
working and not filming
area gone awash thinner
and able really
to "amble" in the class-
partitioned streets of the city
split east west
and the petty violences
as maybe now
intensities or so many flows
regarded with such
internal tension
and external torque
that easy hatred and lovely
disdain training in
typesetting or buildings as
vocation to can't
little utopic touches
of the total design work

making, history,
conditions, actions
under

When the Bubble Pops, Inflate a Utopia Dome

Is it world domination
this amassing and massive
moving of mostly crappy goods
and personal yearnings
or just the soaring speculation
of deeply fucked dot com?
With hard-won individual
anxieties, rights, freedoms, etc.
on a first-name basis
try imagining that you live
in this century (city). Good. Now
park the Sports Utility Vehicle
and circulate freely
amongst the competing cultural
information and traditions
you have access to.
I'm just sort of ("what ever
happened to") sitting here
imagining a world without walls
or *wallpaper**, like "reflexive" or
"second" or "free form"
modernism but with
better stackable chairs
and accredited poetry workshops
for the masses (Jacobsen, Jakobson & Brik).
Trusting in art to help me (why wontcha babe)
get over the blank stare of the commodity
(keep me hangin on). If it is
my hatred of classical music

that will save me
in the end
show me
a better (bitter)
century, more social, less
pharmaceutical and sure of the loss
of causality, after all
these are only ideas, worse (worst)
yet, words
and not people opening
their windows to check
the middle morning weather
(retired postal workers
with heart conditions) in emergent
hardened border Europe
the lyrical working district
that circles the city
"girdles the globe"
"the image of an engine"
"the new mobility
of people and money"
"industry outputs" "Thailand,
Japan and, Time
Warner, Tokyo, Toronto, Turkey, un-
employment, unions, United Kingdom, United
Nations, Uruguay."

Music. Movies

In the Age of Megastructures

Often I am pressured
to return to Khrushchev
the cold moments
of the model kitchen, the shoe removed
in the General Assembly
a time permeated (perma-frosted) with the optimism
of modular stackable habitable
concrete "space frames
with plug-in units"

"Someone Like You"

Dear Capitalism, please
give me a reason
to believe. And then off I go
on the technoscape
not high above but
with pulsing pockets and shopping
opportunities in public space!
This nation is fine if only
it could be in the present
like Peter Sellers (not the "Indian"
Peter Sellers): sorry start again
the movement from the past to the present
was hard, but I got to keep
my car to handle the curly roads
of the ethnoscape: sorry start again:
you are your mode
of production surfing the long waves
of capitalism in a tube
and you lose your bikini top
and only Elvis will
give it back and the small *e*
Levis of your youth *are* your retirement
fund. The summary then:
we are flying your dad in
for a consultation because we
all of us are very disappointed
in your rate at closing today
so borrow my Metrocard and go to
the Freud Museum daily followed

by a coffee in the café
where Lukács read through the cold
organizing winters and forget that form is never more
than a reflection of the relations
of production. As an organizing principle
I'm inept

Sly Consumption Side Sentence

Dear neoliberalism, I
just want to thank you
for letting me
be a mobile
self-reflexive
commodity with agency
putting no pressure
on former state structures
anew, again
till you use me up
consumption side
just like you did
production side with Dad
add an *e*, dead

The Perfect Pure Pop Moment

For global people, for the infinite
touchdown of fleeting capital
whirling overhead
like a helicopter
with a hard-on.
There goes (flows)
my "lust for life" again
Iggy or Avenue B
as I try
to define myself
on design that's "just
in time" annihilated by
a plethora of more or less.
Formal freedoms abound
bound under bonds
of better boundaries. What part of "kiss
my unmanned aerial drone" don't you understand?
Historically defined by expansion, he
hopes to settle down
and raise some children
of his own, long walks through
the long days and waves
of crumbling accumulation
like *Escape from New York*
or *Fort Apache: The Bronx*—a city
bankrupt before
better behavior.
Drop dead
gorgeous

abolition
of private
property
summed
up in
the
single sentence

"Everybody's Happy Nowadays"

I have lived my life
As if in a lament
As if cemented in
A file folder
Of another's devising
Or vision of the future
Much like the now
I can't quite own
To be alone, transnationally
And more
Than a little queasy
Is the chorus
After the burning red-hot
power chords

On

Here comes
the hook (teenage kicks):
"the exploitation
of the many
by the few"
just
got
bigger

APPENDIX A

A Note on the "Forced Thoughts"

This poem was generated by the chance finding of Jackson Mac Low's *From Pearl Harbor Day to FDR's Birthday* in an unlikely bookstore in Del Mar, California in December 1994. At that time the State of California was proposing its racist and xenophobic Bill 187 which sought to restrict rights of "illegal immigrants." Aimed specifically at the Latin American working class whose enforced cheap labour fuels California's economy, this bill reflected a particular tension between "universal" rights (such as health care and education) and the necessity for a reserve army of low-paid workers, as well as the tension of national identity and transnational economies. All the contradictions of the linked system of racism, nationalism, sexism and capitalism were concentrated in this chronotope. *From Pearl Harbor Day to FDR's Birthday* seemed to uncannily capture and comment on this capitalist tension and its contradictions; not primarily from a semantic viewpoint, but from a syntactic and methodological one. Mac Low's use of four-line and three-line stanzas and the short, torqued sentences and utterances within them, in combination with the syllabic collisions of the heteroglot vocabulary, lay bare the overdeterminations within language in a way that seemed to me to mimic the over-determinations and contradictions within Bill 187. Far from being a new mode of realism, *From Pearl Harbor Day to FDR's Birthday* operates as a social fact embedding the contradictions of the relations of production in the economic unit of "North America"; contradictions that, no matter how overdetermined, do not necessarily lead to a positive or more democratic change. That the poems seemed to point so specifically to this condition, and to that moment in California, illuminate the relationship between the dominant modes and relations of production and the modes of production of meaning. Going beyond a reading of context into text, *From Pearl Harbor Day to FDR's Birthday* provided me with a method to approach the contradictions of a particular social moment. Walter Benjamin focused on the production side of culture in his famous essay "The Author as Producer" and it is applicable here: "An author who teaches writers nothing, teaches no one. What matters therefore is the exemplary character of production, which is able first to induce other producers to produce, and second to put an improved apparatus at their disposal." It is toward this end of the transformation of production, that "Forced Thoughts" (a term for a symptom of migraines in which the migraine sufferer is unable to shake a particular thought or progression of thoughts, but a term that could equally apply to ideological interpellation) tries to continue.

Appendix B

When we think we are making fun of the ruling
ideology, we are merely strengthening its hold on us.
—Slavoj Žižek, *Welcome to the Desert of the Real*